A Skateboard
for Alex

written by
Ellen Javernick

illustrated by
Gloria Gedeon

"Cool, my own skateboard!" said Alex as he opened his birthday present. "This is the best present ever."

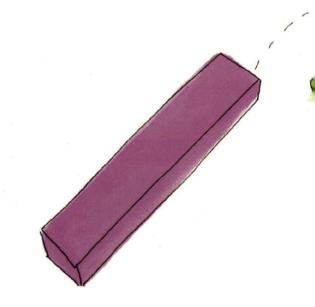

3

Alex grabbed the skateboard and ran out the door.

"Wait!" called Alex's father. "There's more. This box goes with your skateboard."

Alex did not stop.

Alex set his skateboard on the sidewalk. He jumped on and sped off.

"Come back!" called Alex's mother. "We have something else for you."

Alex did not stop.

"Watch me," Alex said. "I can do a wheelie. I can catch some air."

"That is not safe," warned Alex's sister.

Alex did not stop.

Alex spun around and around. He did a flip. He rode his skateboard to a big ramp.

"Not there!" cried Alex's brother.

Alex did not stop.

Alex climbed to the top of the ramp.
"I'm going to drop in," he said.

Everybody screamed, "Stop!"

It was too late. Alex couldn't stop.

Alex wove. He wobbled. He wiped out!

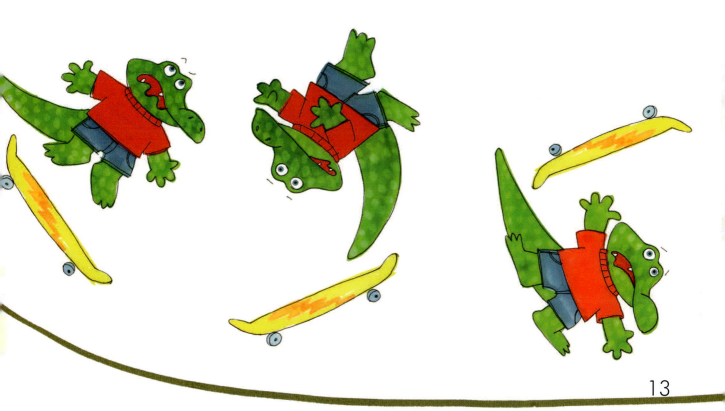

Alex started to cry. "I should have listened when everyone told me to stop."

"Yes, you should have listened," said Alex's mother as she checked for broken bones.

"Yes, you should have listened," said Alex's father as he checked for blood. "You are lucky you do not need stitches," he said.

When they got home Alex opened his second birthday present.

"Cool, my own helmet and pads!" he said. "*This* is the best present ever!"